Copyright ©2021 by Cheong Academy

The right of David Cheong and Cheong Academy as the (

with the Copyright Design and Patents Act of 1988.

MW00928170

All rights reserved under International Copyright Conventions. No part of this publication may be reproduced, stored in a retrieval system, or transmitted, in any form or by any means without prior written permission of the author; nor be otherwise circulated in any form of binding or cover other than that which it is published and without a similar condition including this condition being imposed on the subsequent purchaser.

Version 1.0 February 2020.

Version 2.0 January 2021

Exclusion of Liability and Disclaimer

While every reasonable effort has been made, printing errors may still arise, David Cheong and Cheong Academy and the publisher shall not be held liable for any printing error; typo error or mistake. It is also impossible to predict all the circumstances in which it may be used. Accordingly, neither the author, retailer, nor any other suppliers shall be liable to any person or entity with respect to any loss or damage caused or alleged to be caused by the information contained in or omitted from this publication.

www.passresexam.com
Version 2.0. Copyright reserved by **Cheong Academy Pte Ltd**. DO NOT make copies.

WHO IS THIS BOOK FOR

- This book is for those taking the RES Exam for the **first time** or **retaking it**.

- It is for those who **must pass** the RES exam and are **willing** to work super-hard.

- It is for those who are **stuck** on how to get started to revise for the RES exam

- It is for those who wants a **systematic and progressive plan** to pass the RES exam.

- It is for those who want to learn the **duplicatable steps** to pass the exam from those who have passed the RES exam.

Version 2.0. Copyright reserved by **Cheong Academy Pte Ltd**. DO NOT make copies.

"Twenty years from now you will be more disappointed by the things that you didn't do than by the things you did do. So throw off the bowlines. Sail away from the safe harbour. Catch the trade winds in your sails. Explore. Dream. Discover."

Mark Twain

Version 2.0. Copyright reserved by **Cheong Academy Pte Ltd**. DO NOT make copies.

Table of contents

Who is this book for..2

Acknowledgements 5

Foreword..6

....6

Who is David Cheong?...7

Introduction 9

Your passport to the real estate industry 10

Why This Survival Guide?...11

understand the game 12

Winning starts with your mindset..13

The Pass RES Exam Formula...14

Perceive Rightly..15

Practice Sufficiently 19

The pass res exam 1000-question Rule...20

Plan Strategically 22

A 20-minute truth exercise...26

Do you need a coach?...30

Pass RES Exam Online Revision program..31

Timeline for the res exam 33

Love to study together?..34

GET your Pass RES Exam Swipe File..35

Pass RES Exam Practice Questions Workbooks 36

paper 1 sample practice questions...38

paper 2 sample practice questions...40

Answers to Sample Questions..42

words of encouragement..43

pass res exam checklist..44

ACKNOWLEDGEMENTS

To my **beloved mum, Ruth** ... who believes 100% in me and inspires me dream BIG!

To my **beloved sons, Isaac and Joshua** ... for believing in Daddy and taking adventures with me. You boys are my joy and strength. So blessed to have you both as arrows in my quiver.

To my **real estate mentors** ... Ismail Gafoor, Kelvin Fong, Yong Hock, Alan Lim, Colin Tan, Alvin Low, and Victor Khoo, you guys gave me knowledge, skills and confidence to soar.

To my **PropNex teammates at Alvin Low Division** ... thanks for your friendship and partnership in real estate. You guys make work easier and more fun!

To my **students** ... thank you for trusting me to guide you through your RES Course. We laughed together, we struggled together and sometimes we cried together. Many of you are shining in the industry. You have touched so many lives and transformed families, one at a time. I am so proud of you!

To my **Lord Jesus Christ** ... You are my Shepherd that leads me and restores my soul. You are my Wisdom, Biggest Encourager and my Best Friend. This book would not be possible without your Grace. Thank you so much!!

Version 2.0. Copyright reserved by **Cheong Academy Pte Ltd**. DO NOT make copies.

FOREWORD

I got to know David through a common friend back in 2017 and knew David's passion in RES Training. At the same time, I've also heard many Aspiring Real Estate Salespersons failed their RES exams as many as 8-10 times & some already gave up.

Very rare in this day and age, the key most unique trait about David is he is able to let new agents stay interested, remember key concepts by infusing live example with his curated approach.

I must say he put in a lot of effort preparing for training and hence trainees are seeing almost immediate results. As we know, Time = $. I've heard very good feedback from associates who attended David's RES Course, took action and eventually passed within a very short span of time.

David is certain my "go-to" person whenever an aspiring salesperson seek recommendation

- **ALVIN LOW | ASSOCIATE DISTRICT DIRECTOR | PROPNEX REALTY**

David was my RES lecturer back in 2012.

Being a super kiasu Singaporean, I would sit in the front row and enjoy the interaction with him to make every dollar I paid counts. I was really impressed by his ability to create discussion around the most boring topics. However, what impressed me was that he shared the famous bible verse,

"With great power comes great responsibility"

Oh no, it's from Spiderman's uncle. Anyway, that's something that I least expected from the real estate field where (I thought) people are driven by profit and leave their conscience at home. He shared with us beyond how to pass the RES exam but very practical ways to always do the right thing. I would highly recommend David's book. He will lead you to pass the RES exam with style!

- **TEO CHENG GUAN (Passed <u>1st time</u>!)**

Version 2.0. Copyright reserved by **Cheong Academy Pte Ltd**. DO NOT make copies.

Who is David Cheong?

am an associate real estate trainer with **Life Mastery Academy** teaching the RES Course.

ince 2011, I have taught the RES Course to over 3,000 students. Teaching is my way to give
back to the community and to nurture leaders for the real estate industry.

Find some good tips on passing the RES Course over here:

> *https://www.youtube.com/channel/UCYQdDf-ldRvG4QHRJMKe-VQ*

Please **like, subscribe** and **share** my channel.

You are going find useful information here ☺

am also a practising real estate consultant with **PropNex Realty**, a Singapore home-grown and
GX-listed real estate agency with over 8,000 salespersons. I have a Facebook page at
www.facebook.com/cheongpropertysg. Hope to connect with you over there ☺

Version 2.0. Copyright reserved by **Cheong Academy Pte Ltd**. DO NOT make copies.

Catherine Yap

I wasn't expecting such an interesting course, thinking this will be quite a torture, but am blessed to have you as our trainer, constantly motivating us to do well and study hard. You are a true gem! Much gratitude to you David Cheong and will definitely keep in contact.

Peter Lim

I thoroughly enjoyed David Cheong's lectures! He's knowledgeable, able to communicate concepts and share life examples to bring concepts through.

Tan Yong Qi Jeremy

David Cheong is very meticulous with his lessons and often relates the lesson content with live examples and experiences which eased my understanding on the concepts being taught

Jane Goh

David Cheong has given me in depth knowledge and helped me to absorb the modules. He is passionate for his students' needs.

Jenn

Thanks David Cheong, your classes were very educational esp when you shared real-life stories and experiences, on top of the notes given. Very patient and helpful

Sim San San

David Cheong is well prepared at all times. He checks on students understanding and encourages active participation of everyone in the class constantly

Jas Ng

David Cheong is pragmatic about his views and opinions of this industry. Very much appreciated. I enjoyed his training thoroughly

Fernandez Clint Valentino

David Cheong's lessons has benefitted me and changed my mindset

Jessica Chua

Smooth delivery and able to break it down into "bite-sized" for us to understand

Ivan Ng

David Cheong's anecdotes had given me good practical insights about the real estate industry and his clarification is clear and comprehensive

Elena Siew

Excellent course delivery in terms of content and encouragement for students. The additional information provided by David Cheong will boost confidence and prepare new

Guan-Heng

I have enjoyed very much your teachings. Also learned from many examples that you have provided. Great experience. Many thanks.

Eileen Lee

David Cheong was a very nice and dedicated mentor. Patient with us and gave us a lot of examples to assist us to understand the topics.

Gene Tan

Thank you Mr David Cheong for his invaluable insight through experiences and guiding us toward application rather than blind teaching

Version 2.0. Copyright reserved by **Cheong Academy Pte Ltd**. DO NOT make copies.

I want to **congratulate you** for getting a copy of the Pass RES Exam Survival Guide!

I promise you that it will be totally worth your time.

Take *action and apply the principles* shared in this guide.

What you're going to get out from this guide can massively help you to pass RES exam, whether you are taking RES exam the first time or retaking this exam.

Follow <u>your</u> dream,

David Cheong

9

Version 2.0. Copyright reserved by **Cheong Academy Pte Ltd**. DO NOT make copies.

YOUR PASSPORT TO THE REAL ESTATE INDUSTRY

Passing the RES exam is mandated by CEA (Council of Estate Agencies) before you can apply for the RES License. The license is your passport to the real estate industry.

Why is this license important to you?

Is it to…

- Achieve more income and travel the world?
- Get more recognition?
- Have more time flexibility … get more time with your family?
- Pay for your children's university fee?
- Repair your marriage?
- Get back your health?
- Clear debts?
- Help other people?

Whatever your reason is, it's valid and I am with you.

My mission is simple and clear - To help you **pass the RES exam.**

Let's get started!

Version 2.0. Copyright reserved by **Cheong Academy Pte Ltd**. DO NOT make copies.

WHY THIS SURVIVAL GUIDE?

Failing the RES exam is simply painful. **Very painful** ☹

To some of you, you want to start work asap as a realtor, or else there will be lost opportunities leading to immeasurable loss.

To some of you, it's a waste of your time and money.

I don't want you to see you fail this exam. I believe you do not want to fail too.

This exam has been the biggest obstacle for many people before they can start making income for their family.

After training more than 3,000 students in the RES Course since 2011, I have observed a pattern in students who **passed the RES exams first time** and another pattern in **those who don't**. *These two patterns seem to be happening all the time!*

Whether you're doing the RES exam the first time or retaking it, understanding these two patterns is going to help you!

P.S. This book is not about a magical formula to pass the RES exam. It is for those who are willing to learn the strategies and work hard (***and smart***) to pass the exam.

Version 2.0. Copyright reserved by **Cheong Academy Pte Ltd**. DO NOT make copies.

UNDERSTAND THE GAME

Like a rugby game, you got to understand how the game is played and how to win it.

To pass the RES exam, you need to score at least 60 out of 100.

P.S. There is no bell curve in the passing rate as some people would have you think (I call them the conspiracy theorists).

You may ask, "David, if it is 60/100 to pass, why is it that so many people failed in this exam?" **Simple answer: "This is a pretty difficult exam!"**

While 60/100 sounds simple, it's not easy. If you don't study right, do your drills & plan to win, this exam can be your worst nightmare. This exam will not be a walk in the park.

That's why I wrote this survival guide **to help you!**

Version 2.0. Copyright reserved by **Cheong Academy Pte Ltd**. DO NOT make copies.

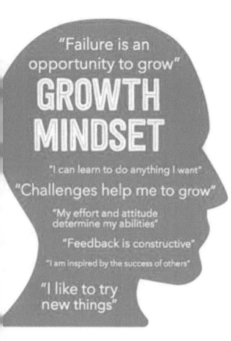
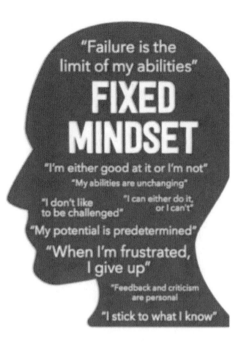

Singapore's real estate laws and policies can sometimes change overnight. Due to COVID-19, the real estate industry has adapted to new ways of doing business and embraced digital transformation. Welcome guys to the new normal.

What is your mindset? **Growth or Fixed?**

In order to pass the RES Exam, it is no longer just acquiring knowledge in class.

Knowledge is still important but what's more important is whether you can <u>apply</u> the knowledge and are you staying <u>relevant</u>?

*P.S. At least 80 percent of the RES exam questions is based on application (**no more rote memorization of facts**). You must understand the real estate concepts and solve real-life questions.*

Version 2.0. Copyright reserved by **Cheong Academy Pte Ltd**. DO NOT make copies.

THE PASS RES EXAM FORMULA

I shared with you earlier the 2 sets of patterns I discovered in my students who passed the exams and those students who kept failing (and they wondered why they failed). The following table shows you the two patterns.

	Students who passed the exam (especially those who passed on their first attempt)	Students who **keep failing the exam**
Level of Understanding	High	Low
Amount of Practice	High	Low
Have A Plan	Yes	No
Have A Coach	Yes	Maybe
Level of Consistency	High	Low
Study in A Group	Yes	Mostly no
Take Notes	All the time, and a lot	Hardly
Ask Questions	Yes, and a lot	Hardly

When I understood the patterns, I went on to formulate the **Pass RES Exam Formula**, to help my students **massively improve their chance to pass the RES exam**. This formula is super easy to remember. Just **3Ps**.

1) **Perceive** Rightly
2) **Practise** Sufficiently
3) **Plan** Strategically

Moving forward, let me share with you.

- Why this is important
- How to do it
- What are the resources that can help you

Version 2.0. Copyright reserved by **Cheong Academy Pte Ltd**. DO NOT make copies.

PERCEIVE RIGHTLY

When you are able to understand the real estate concepts rightly, you are able to apply the knowledge and pick the **best** answer to solve the exam questions.

To illustrate my point, let's try one question together.

Question : The seller of the house has installed a wall-mounted amplifier on the wall, can he take it out after the sale of the house?

    a)   Yes, it is a fitting and can be removed after the sale

    b)   No, it is a fixture, cannot be removed after the sale

    c)   Yes, but the buyer has to compensate the seller

    d)   No, the buyer must give consent before the seller can take it with him

Ask yourself what is the concept that is tested here? **What is your answer?**

Don't go to the next page until you have written down your answer

Your answer is _____

Version 2.0. Copyright reserved by **Cheong Academy Pte Ltd**. DO NOT make copies.

The concept tested here is **The Rule of Fixtures,** which are the general rules of fixtures which property owners (as well as property agents) should be familiar with.

This concept states the **4 ways to ascertain whether an item is a fitting or a fixture** by the way of

1. Intention of the parties

2. Method of Attachment or Annexation

3. Agreement of the parties

4. Items of Attachment

The answer to this question is **(a)**

Version 2.0. Copyright reserved by **Cheong Academy Pte Ltd.** DO NOT make copies.

Tips To Improve Understanding

1. Take your own notes.

Many years ago I have a student from China in my RES Course. Her command of the English language was not strong but she got **strong determination** to pass the exams first time. She took tons of notes in my class (writing them in Chinese). Hey, my lectures were conducted in English!

At the end of the course, I found out that her notes in Chinese are **thicker** than my course textbook that's written in English!

She shared with me that she has no doubt to pass the exam 1st time and she did!

Taking notes can help you stay focused and engaged during your RES Course or also during your revisions for the exam.

2) **Find a suitable environment to study.** Avoid studying at noisy places. It can help you to focus better.

3) **Read your notes / training slides / recent policy changes and property news.** Read with understanding. Read your notes at least 2 times before the exam. Reading can help you to remember better, retain more information and improve your understanding.

4) **Ask Questions.** Read my "Super Talkative Gal" story ☺

Version 2.0. Copyright reserved by **Cheong Academy Pte Ltd**. DO NOT make copies.

The Super Talkative Gal

I have a student who asked me a lot of questions during my class. She would interrupt the class frequently to ask questions. At times, I felt like telling her to ask less questions or give other people a chance to ask questions. It's funny that her classmates do not mind at all. Most of them are happily taking notes or playing with their phones or a few were falling asleep!

I realized that the class actually had the same questions as her, but they do not dare to ask. Maybe it's a typical Singaporean thing – shy to ask question openly. Maybe it's the fear of looking stupid in the public or being judged by others. Since the class don't mind her asking questions, I continued to let her pour out her questions as the class was also learning on her behalf. I know that this super talkative gal didn't do much practice questions and went for the exam anyway. How do I know that? **She told me herself.** Guess what?

She passed the RES exam at her **first** attempt!

What's the morale of this story?

Be engaged. Ask lots of questions.

Why? Because that will help you a ton to get the right understanding of real estate concepts and apply them correctly during the exams. Start to discuss your questions with your RES trainer or an industry leader to clear all your doubts. Or get into a study group to ask your questions and get answers from your fellow study-mates.

☺ *Whenever I share her story, it will put a smile on my face. I am so proud of her.*

Version 2.0. Copyright reserved by **Cheong Academy Pte Ltd**. DO NOT make copies.

If you want to be a professional musician, would it be sufficient for you to just play the instrument once a month or twice a month?

I believe you would say no, isn't it.

Likewise for the RES exam, **you must do a lot of practice questions to succeed.**

Version 2.0. Copyright reserved by **Cheong Academy Pte Ltd**. DO NOT make copies.

THE PASS RES EXAM 1000-QUESTION RULE

As a guideline, I recommend you do **at least 1,000 questions** to prepare yourself for this challenging exam.

To make it clearer for you.

- Do at least 500 questions for Paper 1

- Do at least 500 questions for Paper 2

You can do more, but you should not do less than 1,000 questions.

Practice breeds clarity and confidence

Practice helps you to test out your understanding of the concepts, to see if you have understood them correctly or not.

P.S. Don't just read your notes without practicing the questions. Sometimes, you can choose to do your practice questions first and then go back to your notes to read in depth. In this way, you might be able to understand your notes better. See if this works for you. ☺

Version 2.0. Copyright reserved by **Cheong Academy Pte Ltd**. DO NOT make copies.

PRACTICE UP-TO-DATE QUESTIONS ONLY

Some questions are no longer applicable anymore in today's context. E.g. Some of the HDB policies or loan requirements have changed recently. If you are doing those out-dated questions, you will get muddled up with the new policies!

GET ALL **1,200** PRACTICE QUESTIONS

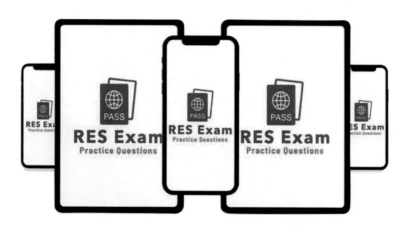

Go to www.passresexam.com/store to get the practice questions in **Ebook (i.e. PDF) format.**

Simply choose whether you want questions for Paper 1 or Paper 2 or both, make payment and you will get the download links to access the eBooks immediately. Answers are provided.

P.S. PRACTICE UP-TO-DATE QUESTIONS ONLY

P.S.S. If you want to get the paperback books, please go to www.amazon.com to purchase them.

Search "pass res exam david cheong" at amazon.com.

Version 2.0. Copyright reserved by **Cheong Academy Pte Ltd**. DO NOT make copies.

Having a good plan is only half the battle done, the other half is execution.

I have observed that people who failed the RES exam (and often in their endeavours) is not because they do not know what they are supposed to do.

*They know what to do, they have the knowledge, <u>**but they don't take action.**</u>*

If we can be honest, we have all lost to the monsters of procrastination, laziness and lack of self-control. (including the author of this guidebook. I almost didn't want to publish this book! Ok, are you glad that I got it published? ☺)

Sometimes, we want everything to be perfect (or a perfect day) before we start to study, to start doing the practice questions, etc.

Seriously ask yourself, *what is holding you back from getting started?*

Ok, I understand you got kids to attend to.

Ok, I understand you got household or your other work to get done with.

For some of you, you are not in the right mood to study!

(I can almost hear your laughing, giggling and sighing...)

Hey, I understand you because I have done it all. *Getting started can be hard.* ☺

"Hey David, Life happens and I cannot go on anymore..."

I get it but I still want to encourage you to stay calm, **pick yourself up** and get work done.

Yes, you can and you have to.

Version 2.0. Copyright reserved by **Cheong Academy Pte Ltd**. DO NOT make copies.

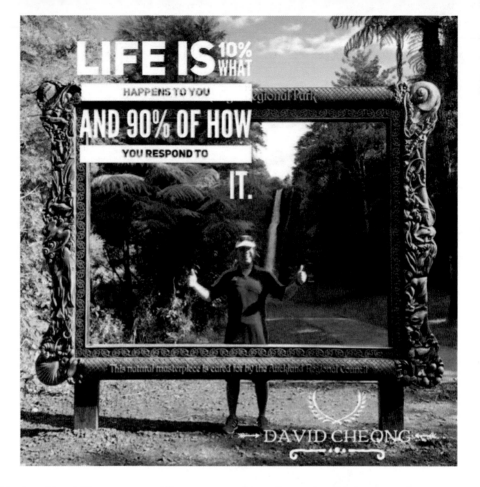

My dear friend, I hope you can allow me to push you forward and help you make progress, *regardless of your circumstances.*

I believe in you. I am praying for you!

It's never too late to get started.

One step at a time. Ok?

Version 2.0. Copyright reserved by **Cheong Academy Pte Ltd**. DO NOT make copies.

I am going to give you a powerful tip. Are you ready?

Start your revision even if you don't feel like it. For just 5 minutes.

If you feel like continuing the work after 5 minutes, go ahead. If not, you just stop.

Is that fair?

Scientific research has shown that 80% of the people who got started will continue to do their work beyond the 5 minutes. Do you know why you don't want to get started and looking for excuses? We call this procrastination. **Because you are stressed.**

If you are interested why I said that, google **"Mel Robbins 5-Second Rule"**. She explains it better.

There's a scientific finding to prove that procrastination is due to stress. Hey, it's not your fault and there's a way out to beat this monster. It's called the 5-second rule. For now just trust me by doing a countdown mentally from 5 and start doing right away.

5, 4, 3, 2, 1, start … do for 5 minutes.

Version 2.0. Copyright reserved by **Cheong Academy Pte Ltd**. DO NOT make copies.

A 20-MINUTE TRUTH EXERCISE

Please answer these 5 questions honestly.

Take your time. Don't rush through it. *Go ahead to play some inspiring music to help you to reflect and to listen to your own heart. You deserve an honest time with yourself. If you can, write down how you feel in the spaces below. No long answers is required.*

1. **Why do you have to pass the RES exam?**

2. **What's holding you back from your dreams?**

3. **What keeps you awake at night?** (Your dreams or your fears?)

4. **What are you going to <u>do differently</u> this time to pass the RES exam?**

5. **When you pass the RES Exam, what are your possibilities?**

Version 2.0. Copyright reserved by **Cheong Academy Pte Ltd**. DO NOT make copies.

Please do not proceed to the next page until you are done with this exercise.

This exercise really matters. Do this for yourself, for your family and for your future.

Version 2.0. Copyright reserved by **Cheong Academy Pte Ltd**. DO NOT make copies.

Version 2.0. Copyright reserved by **Cheong Academy Pte Ltd**. DO NOT make copies.

How do you feel when you are doing this exercise?

I did this exercise some time ago. For me, *I felt sick and tired of feeling sick and tired.*

I wanted change. I want to change myself.

To me, change is difficult, don't change also difficult.

So I decided to change. I chose progress. It was not easy but it has been rewarding for me.

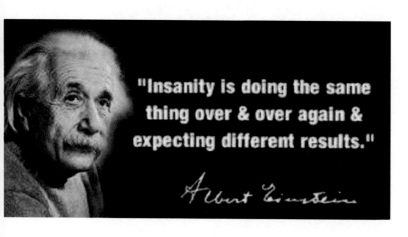

Through this reflection, I hope you understand yourself better. I hope you saw your preferred future and your possibilities. This exercise is to awaken the champion in you.

Please understand this exercise is not for you to dwell in self-pity or blame others or to blame yourself!

I want to inspire you to lead you!

Version 2.0. Copyright reserved by **Cheong Academy Pte Ltd**. DO NOT make copies.

DO YOU NEED A COACH?

Do you remember Joseph Schooling?

He is Singapore's "Golden Boy" who has beaten the mighty Michael Phelps in the Olympics 2016 (Men's 100m Butterfly) and won the 1st Olympics Gold medal for Singapore's history.

Does talented Joseph Schooling have a coach? You bet!

People who **must succeed** recognize their need to be inspired, challenged, disciplined and accountable to someone who can help them to be their best version for themselves.

I have my own coaches and you need yours too.

Your coach does not necessarily have to be me, it can be your RES Course trainer or someone whom you respect in the real estate industry. Please stay accountable to him or her, until at least you have passed this RES exam. Ok?

What if I could show you how to <u>study less</u> and <u>discover key-areas</u> for the exams, so that you <u>don't over-study</u> and <u>don't waste time</u>?

Don't waste your time and monies to retake another exam. Failing the coming exam means waiting 4 long months for the next round of exam.

P.S. There are only 3 rounds of RES Exam every year – in February, June and October.

Version 2.0. Copyright reserved by **Cheong Academy Pte Ltd**. DO NOT make copies.

PASS RES EXAM ONLINE REVISION PROGRAM

This is a systematic and progressive online training to help you cover all key areas for the RES Exam. It is to get you ready for "D-Day"!

Never leave your revision to the last minute. You will go into the panic mode.

*Studying 1 hour daily is better than trying to study 10 hours of study in one day. The **law of diminishing returns** takes effect when we do something for prolonged hours. Your brain is unable to absorb more after some time. **Take one step at a time. Just be consistent.***

In the Pass RES Exam online revision program, I have pre-recorded videos for you to cover all the exam topics systematically. With each "bite-sized" lesson, I will also give you the accompanying practice questions. You can do this program anywhere and anytime.

New! You can check out training **excerpts** from this program at my YouTube channel

https://www.youtube.com/channel/UCYQdDf-ldRvG4QHRJMKe-VQ

Version 2.0. Copyright reserved by **Cheong Academy Pte Ltd**. DO NOT make copies.

The **Pass RES Exam online revision program** is highly recommended for people who need **extra guidance and coaching** after their RES Course.

It's most suitable for people who

⇒ recognize a need for a coach to help them to be better

⇒ must pass this exam

⇒ don't want to waste time figuring everything out themselves

⇒ detest wasting money and time to retake the exam

⇒ must start work asap as a realtor to make more income or else there will be lost opportunities leading to immeasurable loss

⇒ want to study together

⇒ want to be accountable to someone in their Learning Journey

*P.S. As a member of this program, **you can send me your questions directly**.*

> *Enrol now for this program at*
> *www.passresexam.com/revision*

Version 2.0. Copyright reserved by **Cheong Academy Pte Ltd**. DO NOT make copies.

TIMELINE FOR THE RES EXAM

I hope you are aware of the timeline from the point you embark on the journey to take the RES Course to the point you get your RES License. Again this timeline can be shorter or longer depending on factors like when are you going to take the next exam, when you pass the RES exam and the final approval timeline by CEA

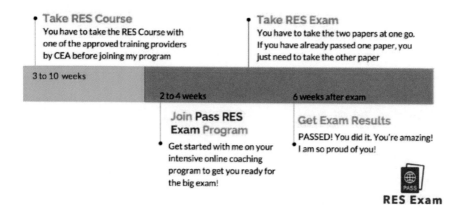

1. If you want to be a part-time property agent and currently holding on to a job, the length of timeline should not affect you significantly. My assumption is that you have time and regular income on your side. No problem.

2. If you want to be a full-time property agent and currently holding on to a job, I strongly advise you **not to quit your job too early** as the due process needed to get your real estate licence can take quite a while.

That's why failing the coming round of exam is painful because you have to wait for another 4 long months to retake the exam. And pay another round of exam fees.

Not to say the wasted opportunities.

P.S. After you pass your RES exam, you can go to your real estate agency of choice to sign an agreement letter with them. Your agency will help you to submit your application to apply for your real estate salesperson license. CEA's approval takes up to 6 weeks because this time, they are doing their due diligence to check if the applicant is deem to be "fit and proper" join the industry.

Version 2.0. Copyright reserved by **Cheong Academy Pte Ltd**. DO NOT make copies.

LOVE TO STUDY TOGETHER?

Join our community of fellow students who are taking the RES exam.

As a member of the Pass RES Exam online revision program, you will get access to our study group on a **private WhatsApp group**.

This is a community where you can share, learn and develop great friendships. Post your questions here and get them answered by your peers or by me personally.

Many of your fellow classmates will become your frontline of real estate co-broking partners when you get your license and start work in the industry. I see that happening all the time. Working with people you know is much easier, faster and fun!

Version 2.0. Copyright reserved by **Cheong Academy Pte Ltd**. DO NOT make copies.

GET YOUR PASS RES EXAM SWIPE FILE

⇒ What if you can complete all your revision in 10 days using this swipe file?

⇒ Confused about "what to study", "where to start from" and you want to get it right?

⇒ How often do you find yourself saying: "I wish I knew what are the key areas to focus on for the exam!"

⇒ Thinking of how you can revise for the whole exam so that you can pass the exam within the next month?

⇒ **What if there is a swipe file that you can deploy immediately to help you take a giant step to pass the res exam?**

I hear you and I am pleased to share with you

⇒ A guide to help you to study faster and pass the RES exam.

⇒ A blueprint to help you revise in a systematic and progressive way

⇒ A quick way to get all the key-points revised for Paper 1 and Paper 2.

⇒ All the key-points note-taking have been done for you ☺

⇒ Those who failed their res exam would have **paid the full price** to get this swipe file a few months ago.

PURCHASE IT AT **WWW.PASSRESEXAM.COM/STORE**

Version 2.0. Copyright reserved by **Cheong Academy Pte Ltd**. DO NOT make copies.

I hate to nag but this is so important.

My recommendation is for you to do **1,000 practice questions** before you go for your RES exam.

- **Do at least 500 questions for Paper 1**
- **Do at least 500 questions for Paper 2**

Students who passed the exam (**many on their first attempt**) did a ton of practise questions. They have **practised sufficiently** and hence able to understand the real estate concepts and apply them well.

To help you with that, I have curated **1,200 practice questions** and compiled them into **2 workbooks**.

One workbook for **Paper 1 (640 questions)** and one workbook for **Paper 2 (560 questions)**.

After you have completed all the questions in the workbooks, you should be sufficiently ready for your exams. All our questions are **up-to-date** and many of them are challenging.

Answers are provided.

GET YOUR PRACTICE QUESTIONS (EBOOK VERSION) AT WWW.PASSRESEXAM.COM/STORE

P.S. PRACTICE UP-TO-DATE QUESTIONS ONLY

P.S.S. If you want to get the paperback books, please go to www.amazon.com to purchase them. Search "pass res exam david cheong" at amazon.com.

Version 2.0. Copyright reserved by **Cheong Academy Pte Ltd**. DO NOT make copies.

Jennifer Siew Fun Loh is with **David Cheong.** •••

21 h · 🔒

Since my son had passed , so this two books need to pass to someone else le !! Haha ...Thks David

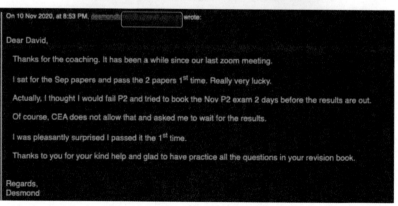

On 10 Nov 2020, at 8:53 PM, desmond[ ] wrote:

Dear David,

Thanks for the coaching. It has been a while since our last zoom meeting.

I sat for the Sep papers and pass the 2 papers 1st time. Really very lucky.

Actually, I thought I would fail P2 and tried to book the Nov P2 exam 2 days before the results are out.

Of course, CEA does not allow that and asked me to wait for the results.

I was pleasantly surprised I passed it the 1st time.

Thanks to you for your kind help and glad to have practice all the questions in your revision book.

Regards,
Desmond

Version 2.0. Copyright reserved by **Cheong Academy Pte Ltd**. DO NOT make copies.

PAPER 1 SAMPLE PRACTICE QUESTIONS

1. **Which of the following statement is untrue?**

   (a) A change in price will not affect the quantity supplied in an inelastic supply situation.
   (b) Government's land sale programme is an important source of supply
   (c) Property characteristics such as age, height are important demand factors
   (d) Buyers' market is a situation where we have more demand than supply

2. **Which of the following example is not a Licence?**

   (a) A professional singer who is performing at the Esplanade Concert Hall has the right to use the Artists Room during the week of her performance
   (b) Nancy who went to her boss' condominium to collect his mail and her boss' permission to use the swimming pool in the condo
   (c) Robert has the right to park his car in a HDB multi storey car park when he visits his friend at his HDB flat
   (d) Alan has the right to use his neighbour's driveway to reach his home as it is the only way for him to access his property

3. **Jack and Jill are 'next door' neighbours of a pair of semi-detached houses. Jack loves to invite his friends to his friends for barbecue over the weekends; while Jill loves gardening. Over a period of time, the smoke from the weekends' barbecues caused the leaves of a tree Jill had planted very near to Jack's barbecue pit to turn bad. What rights does Jill have as the land owner against Jack for causing damage to her tree?**

   (a) Jill can go to the court to apply for an injunction against Jack's frequent barbecues at his own house
   (b) Jill can go to the court to apply for a restrictive covenant to be imposed upon Jack's land against smokes from blowing out of his land into Jill's land
   (c) Jill can complain to the National Park authority for action to be taken against Jack for causing damage to the natural flora
   (d) Jill can go to the court to seek the court's declaration that the smoke was a nuisance and seek compensation from Jack.

4. **Developer installed an aircon on the 3' d storey of the building and the aircon protrudes out onto the main road.**

   (a) Developer would have to seek grant of temporary occupation licence to regularize the encroachment
   (b) Developer would have to seek grant for State Lease to allow the aircon to maintain
   (c) Developer would have to seek grant of sale of remnant land on the part that the aircon protrudes out
   (d) Developer need not do anything for the aircon is part of the building although it protrudes out onto the main road.

Version 2.0. Copyright reserved by **Cheong Academy Pte Ltd.** DO NOT make copies.

5. 'A' left property to 3 daughters after he passed away 20 years ago. Throughout the years, 3 daughters passed away one after the other. The property is now owned by the youngest daughter. 'A' assigned his property by:

   (a) Will, after death
   (b) Will, upon death
   (c) Trust, after death
   (d) Trust, upon death

6. Two weeks after taking the Option to Purchase (OTP) granted by property seller David, Simon decided to proceed with the purchase; but as he was running short of time before the OTP expired in an hour's time, Simon sent David a short message service (SMS) message through his iPhone to inform David of the decision to exercise the Option. However, the next day (15th day after the date written on the OTP) David served a notice of termination to Simon claiming that the Option has lapsed as he did not receive any consideration from the buyer. Can Simon sue David for breach of contract?

   (a) Yes, Simon has performed his part of the contract by informing David of his intention to go ahead with the purchase
   (b) Yes, an electronic means of communication constitutes an act of acceptance of the contractual terms
   (c) Though his intention was conveyed via electronic means, Simon must still meet all the ingredients of a contract including providing the consideration before the Option lapsed
   (d) No, Singapore courts do not accept electronic means of communication as act of acceptance

7. Adrian (Mr A), a real estate salesperson, is having coffee with his client Betty (Ms B). A friend of Betty's, Carol (Ms C) dropped by and asked Mr A about the property market. Mr A expressed a gloomy outlook for the market. On hearing that, Ms C proceeded to sell her property herself. However, she soon realized that her house could fetch a higher price. Ms C was furious and wanted to sue Mr A under tort of negligence.

   (a) Yes, under Tort Ms C need not have a contractual relationship with the defendant Mr A; she needed only to prove that Mr A ought to have exercised care when giving his view on the market, knowing that Ms C would rely on what he said
   (b) Yes, the Tort of Negligence basically protect innocent house owners against all forms of economic losses resulting from professional negligence, e.g. when real estate salespersons advised house owners
   (c) No, Mr A was merely giving his personal opinion on the property market
   (d) No, there were no contractual obligations between the two parties

8. When the landlord repossesses the property because of tenant's default rent, the landlord is exercising his right of _____

9. Foreigners who own landed properties at _____ is not subject to any minimum physical occupation period.

10. Foreigners who wish to buy restricted properties will need to get approval from _____ Unit

Version 2.0. Copyright reserved by Cheong Academy Pte Ltd. DO NOT make copies.

PAPER 2 SAMPLE PRACTICE QUESTIONS

1. Jackson has an existing Service Agreement with a landlord. At the lapse of the Tenancy Agreement, the landlord told Jackson that he would not be paying Jackson any commission for finding the next tenant as Jackson will continue to enjoy the Service Agreement fee on a monthly basis. Can Jackson then collect commission from the incoming tenant since the landlord is not paying him commission?

   (a) Yes, there is no conflict of interest as the Service Agreement is not for estate agency work
   (b) No, that would amount to dual representation
   (c) No, Jackson is already getting paid by the landlord on a monthly basis
   (d) No, as a real estate salesperson Jackson can only be paid by one party regardless of the nature of work he is rendering

2. Mr Lim of Blk 217 Punggol Drive who has stayed in his BTO flat for 4 years, receives a flyer that claims "We can help you SELL your flat before 5 years". Is the salesperson allowed to claim that?

   (a) Yes, as he has experience selling flats during Minimum Occupation Period for special cases
   (b) Yes, as he heard from his fellow salesperson that it can be done
   (c) No, it is circumventing HDB's ruling
   (d) No, salesperson can only sell flats that are 5 years and older

3. Which of the following phrase(s) salesperson cannot use in their advertisements?
   (i) No co-broking
   (ii) Already co-broke
   (iii) No agents
   (iv) 0.5% co-broking fee
   (v) Buyer only
   (vi) Buyer pays 1% commission

   (a) All but (vi)
   (b) All but (v)
   (c) All but (iv)
   (d) All but (iii)

4.
   (i) During an auction, buyers compete with each other in the open
   (ii) The Auctioneer can choose not to accept the highest bidder even if the bid if above the reserve price

   (a) Only (i) is correct
   (b) Only (ii) is correct
   (c) Both are correct
   (d) Both are wrong

Version 2.0. Copyright reserved by **Cheong Academy Pte Ltd**. DO NOT make copies.

5. New Life Church is looking for a space to rent for their services, what are their option/s available?

(i)   Townhouse
(ii) Shop within a shopping mall
(iii) Space within a B1 Industrial Building (with approval)
(iv) Bungalow in Upper Thomson Road

(a) (i) and (ii)
(b) (iii) and (iv)
(c) (ii) only
(d) (iii) only

6. Which of the following situation is an unfair practice?

(a) Salesperson knows that the property is under acquisition and kept quiet about it.
(b) Developer printed the size of the apartment wrongly in the brochure. The brochure has a disclaimer clause.
(c) Advertisement printed with words "artist impression" showing that the building is painted white, but turn out that the building is painted with multi-colours instead.
(d) All of the above

7. Property is sold subject to Purchaser's solicitors receiving satisfactory replies to all requisitions sent by them to the various relevant competent authorities. Which of the following is not one of the competent authorities?

(a) Inland Revenue Authority of Singapore
(b) Building and Construction Authority
(c) Singapore Land Authority
(d) Ministry of Environment and Water Resources

8. Sellers and buyers must use the HDB _____ Option to Purchase as the form of contract in the transaction. Any other agreements and supplementary agreements relating to the sale or purchase of flat are not valid.

9. Rental income refers to the full amount of rent and related payments landlord receive when the property is rented out. This includes rent of the premises, furniture, fittings and _____.

10. Work Permit Holders from _____, Marine and Process sectors must be Malaysians before they are allowed to rent an HDB flat.

Version 2.0. Copyright reserved by **Cheong Academy Pte Ltd**. DO NOT make copies.

ANSWERS TO SAMPLE QUESTIONS

Paper 1		Paper 2	
1	d	1	a
2	d	2	c
3	d	3	c
4	a	4	a
5	d	5	d
6	c	6	a
7	c	7	c
8	forfeiture	8	Prescribed
9	Sentosa Cove	9	Maintenance
10	Land Dealings Approval	10	Construction

Version 2.0. Copyright reserved by **Cheong Academy Pte Ltd**. DO NOT make copies.

WORDS OF ENCOURAGEMENT

"Always believe that something wonderful is about to happen."

"To uncover your true potential, you must first find your own limits and then you have to have the courage to blow past them." - Picabo Street

"Everything that happens helps you grow, even if it's hard to see right now."

"Sometimes you've got to be able to listen to yourself and be okay with no one else understanding."

"The beautiful thing about life is that you can always grow, change and get better. You aren't defined by your past."

"You are strong enough to start again."

"You are allowed to take your time, to grow in your own beautiful way."

"It takes a lot of courage to push through hard times. Never give up. Good things are coming your way."

"Sometimes the place you are used to is not the place you belong."

"The rest of my life is going to be the best of my life."

Don't allow your wounds to turn you into a person you are not. - Paulo Coelho

"Your problem isn't the problem. Your reaction is the problem."

"You will go through pain in your life, but how you choose to respond to it is your choice."

"Count your blessings, not your problems."

"Vision without execution is just hallucination." - Henry Ford

"You do not have to have it all figured out to move forward."

"Life has many different chapters. One bad chapter doesn't mean it's the end of the book."

"I may not be there yet, but I'm closer than I was yesterday."

"Every day may not be good, but there is something good in every day."

"I am not a product of my circumstances. I am a product of my decisions." - Stephen Covey

Version 2.0. Copyright reserved by **Cheong Academy Pte Ltd**. DO NOT make copies.

( )   Perceive Rightly - Understand Concepts

( )   Practice Sufficiently - Do 1,000 questions

( )   Plan Strategically - Get A Plan / Coach

( )   Get Pass RES Exam Practice Workbooks

( )   Get Pass RES Exam Swipe File

( )   Join Pass RES Exam Online Revision Program

( )   Study as a Group

( )   Pray! Ask God for wisdom and grace.

GET ALL YOUR RES EXAM RESOURCES AT WWW.PASSRESEXAM.COM/STORE

Version 2.0. Copyright reserved by **Cheong Academy Pte Ltd**. DO NOT make copies.

Made in the USA
Las Vegas, NV
22 June 2021

25243206R00029